Summary

of DR. MIKE DOW'S

THE BRAIN FOG FIX

Reclaim Your Focus, Memory, and joy in just 3 Weeks

Master in 20 Minutes

With **Bern Bolo**, The Bathroom Genius

Please Note: This is a summary of *"The Brain Fog Fix: Reclaim Your Focus, Memory, and Joy in Just 3 Weeks"* by *Dr. Mike Dow.*

Feel free to send me an email. My publisher filters these emails but I do get them. bern_bolo@awesomeauthors.org Good news is always welcome.

About the Publisher

Epiphany Printing is a member of the **BLVNP Incorporated Group,** 340 S. Lemon #6200, Walnut, CA 91789, info@blvnp.com / legal@blvnp.com

DISCLAIMER

The purpose of this summary is to provide the necessary information found in the original book, as discussed by the author of the original book, to busy readers who may not have enough time to read the original book. The author of this summary does not intend to plagiarise (as the original book's author is mentioned and credited repeatedly) or reprint all the information that is otherwise available to the original book. You are urged to read the original book, *The Brain Fog Fix* by *Dr. Mike Dow*. This summary is available anytime for you if you don't have much time or if you want to understand the key concepts. This summary is meant to complement and amplify the original book.

The Brain Fog Fix

: Reclaim your Focus, Memory,
and Joy in Just 3 Weeks
"Dr. Mike Dow"

A 20-Minute Summary of
"The Brain Fog Fix: Reclaim your Focus,
Memory, and Joy in Just 3 Weeks"
by Dr. Mike Dow

Summary by: Bern Bolo

ISBN: 978-1-68030-637-8

Table of Contents

***

Preface

Dr. Mike Dow is an author, psychotherapist, TV host of several health shows, and a real authority on several issues in psychology. He holds a doctorate degree in psychology and a license to practice psychotherapy. He published his first book in 2011, the *Diet Rehab*, which is currently available in three languages.

The Brain Fog Fix is *Dr. Mike Dow*'s latest book. It deals with an issue that a lot of the middle to late adults in the world relate to: the mood and thinking disturbances that are not severe enough to be classified as a disease but are enough to affect one's daily functioning – or simply called *the brain fog*.

He dedicates *The Brain Fog Fix* to everyone, including his own family members, as he knows how damaging unstable thoughts and moods can be. Not only can they put you in a perpetual state of unhappiness and inefficiency, they can also damage your relationship with yourself and with the important people in your life. *The Brain Fog Fix* will not only help you deal with the regular stresses of life but also assist you in getting over those moments that could leave you in downright misery.

Dr. Mike Dow aims to help you prevent or fight depression, anxiety, brain fog, and other symptoms that indicate cognitive impairment through *The Brain Fog Fix*. Through this book, he hopes to assist you in attaining a fuller and happier life.

The changes that you will undergo will be subtle and seemingly insignificant. Know that these changes are achievable. They are not particularly difficult but they definitely need to be implemented with strict discipline.

Eat right. Exercise regularly. Relieve your stress. Sleep soundly. Connect with people and with a greater source of energy. Let *Dr. Mike Dow*'s 21-day program help you *reclaim your focus, memory, and joy.*

One
THE FOG AND ITS SOURCE

"You are on the bus and you really need to fart.
The music is really loud, so you time your farts with the beat.
A couple of songs later you start to feel better.
As you leave the bus, people are really giving you the evil eye,
and that's when you remember...
...you've been listening to your iPod!"

More and more people experience a chronic cognitive and mood problem every year. People call it *brain fog*, *depression*, or *ADHD* (Attention Deficit Hyperactivity Disorder). When you have this, you do not feel like yourself. You feel frustrated, miserable, or anxious.

This problem is not just about your mental or emotional state but also your physiological state. Your hormones have the power to affect your mood and thinking. Specifically, these hormones are:

1. *Serotonin* – makes you optimistic, calm, and confident

   A very low amount of this can cause you get anxiety, depression, sleep problems, and others. Using antidepressants to combat the lows will make you prone to dependence, brain fog, and reduced sexual desire and function.

2. *Dopamine* – makes you excited and motivated

   A very low amount will make you anhedonic; you will feel as though nothing ever excites you and life has no meaning. An unusually high amount of this will make you lose focus; you may even experience compulsion and addiction. Drinking caffeine and stimulants to counterbalance the high may lead to untoward incidences.

3. *Cortisol* – known as the stress hormone

   A cortisol imbalance either exhausts you or revs you up too much that you may get too weak during the day and restless during the night. An unusually high level of this can inhibit dopamine and serotonin. If you turn to medications because of this, you may get too dependent on them.

Factors that can affect the release of these three hormones include wrong diet, inadequate sleep, minimal exercise, constant stress, overindulgence in social media, non-existent personal connection, and a lack of meaning in life. You may suddenly find that you are too exhausted and too cranky to get anything done and that nothing motivates or inspires you.

Relying on caffeine, sleeping aids, antianxiety medications, and the wrong kinds of food can worsen the situation. In fact, they simply result to more problems.

The social media is where you try to find connection. In truth, it only promotes isolation.

People's lives are so busy nowadays; no one makes time for religious or spiritual practices anymore.

Everyone is so busy *doing* that they forget simply *being*.

Choose the natural approach over pills to combat problems. Make changes in your diet, sleep and other lifestyle choices. You may think that these do not matter, but they have a very large influence on your overall well-being. These simple and subtle changes will help you achieve the balance you need to live your life.

The *three weeks* featured in *The Brain Fog Fix* is the healing period necessary to normalize the amounts of these chemicals in your body. Practically, it has two principles:

1. Give the brain what it needs:
    a. Right diet
    b. Exercise
    c. Adequate sleep
    d. Healthy circadian rhythms
    e. Time for relaxation and restoration
    f. Purpose and meaning
    g. Spirituality
    h. Connection with something larger than yourself

2. Remove the obstacles that can block the brain's optimal functioning:
    a. Sugar, high-fructose corn syrup, and artificial sweeteners
    b. Processed white flour
    c. Too many inflammatory foods, including conventionally grown meat, unhealthy fats, and many artificial ingredients and preservatives
    d. An imbalance of omega-6 and omega-3 fats
    e. Excessive use of brain-altering substances, such as caffeine, alcohol, and recreational drugs
    f. Many medications, including unnecessary antidepressants, antianxiety agents, ADHD stimulants, sleep aids, and painkillers
    g. Overexposure to the *blue light* of electronic screens, including of computers, TV, and phones
    h. Bombardment with diverse tasks and inputs, such as an ongoing flood of texts, emails, and social media, such as *Twitter*, *Facebook*, and *Instagram*
    i. Too much time spent in doing activities that do not feel meaningful and purposeful, whether they're for compliance with obligation (work and family duties) or for entertainment (shopping or gambling)

To promote the fixing and improve your mood and thinking, the 21-day period is divided into three phases:

Week 1: The 7-Day *Mood* Revolution

Week 2: The 7-Day *Energy* Revolution

Week 3: The 7-Day *Spirit* Revolution

Before getting into the first phase, you must understand the impact of wrong lifestyle choices on your health; not only do they set you up for physical illnesses but they also promote mental and emotional decline.

Two
MOOD AND FOOD

"Beans, beans, they're good for your heart
The more you eat, the more you fart
The more you fart, the happier/better you feel
So let's eat beans with every meal."

CARBOHYDRATES

Carbohydrate is an important part of your diet as it provides the necessary energy to your body, most especially to the brain. However, having too much of it can lead to obesity and certain diseases. It can also affect your brain chemistry and can result to dementia as it is known to be a pro-inflammatory. It is also known to cause a condition called *insulin resistance*, which has been implicated to result to Alzheimer's disease.

In other words, too much blood sugar can lead to cognitive decline.

To prevent all these, you need to make some modifications in your diet and regulate your intake of carbohydrate by switching to healthier options:

1. *Use no artificial sweeteners* – such as diet sodas. Artificial sweeteners may not add calories, but they cannot give you the amount of nutrients your brain needs.
2. *Do blood-sugar swaps* by replacing foods which can cause a sharp increase in your blood sugar with complex carbohydrates. Here are some examples:
    a. When cooking pasta, try to substitute it with zucchini or spaghetti squash noodles, or bulk up the dish with broccoli or cauliflower. And do not overcook the pasta.
    b. When eating out, try to have your bread *shelled out*, to cut the carbs in half. Order spinach, tomato, olives, and green peppers.

   c. Before eating pizza, eat a big plate of salad with vinegar and olive oil, to reduce pizza consumption to one to two slices.
3. *Eating the following food* will promote regulation of blood sugar:
   a. *Cinnamon.* In making coffee, use cinnamon instead of sugar as it has anti-inflammatory and antioxidant effects.
   b. *Raw or partially cooked vegetables.* The fiber content counteracts the blood-sugar spikes.
   c. *Vinegar.* It helps lower blood sugar by preventing starch from turning into sugar.
   d. *Tea.* It helps reduce the amount of glucose absorbed by the intestines.
   e. *Red Wine.* This is advisable for those who do not have a history of alcoholism as it lessens intestinal absorption and liver production of glucose.
4. *Follow the 80/20 rule*: Eighty percent of the time, eat complex carbohydrates while 20% of the time, let loose a little bit.

FATS

Fats can also hugely affect your mental health. It is not always bad for the body. In fact, monounsaturated fats, such as olive oil, and fats with high omega-3 can go a long way in preserving the brain.

Omega-3

As it is anti-inflammatory, it helps preserve brain function and prevent depression, stress, and anxiety. It can help prevent a myriad of lifestyle diseases and can also help counteract cancer. As the body cannot produce it on its own, it is necessary to include food rich with Omega-3 in your diet. There are three types of Omega-3 fatty acids:

1. ALA

It is the oil obtained from vegetables; it still has to be converted into the two other types of Omega-3 to maximize benefits.

2. DHA

   It is mostly found in fish, seaweed, and DHA-enriched milk; it promotes cognition and brain development.

3. EPA

   This is also found in seafood; it can improve and stabilize your mood.

It is important to increase your intake of Omega-3, and it is equally important to decrease your intake of Omega-6, a pro-inflammatory fatty acid. It can be found in many varieties of processed foods and refined vegetable oils, which are very rampant nowadays. Regulating the intake of these two kinds of fatty acid can help you maintain hormonal balance.

This is done by increasing your intake of shrimp, scallop, and fish. But remember to choose the kinds that are caught in their natural state (in the sea), not those that are cultured and raised in the farm. The latter has a higher content of Omega-6 than of Omega-3.

Olive Oil

Not all fats are harmful to the body. In fact, olive oil has been proven to help people think and feel better. It also has anti-inflammatory compounds, which can help prevent dementia and depression.

To maximize your intake of olive oil, spray it on your bread for breakfast, sprinkle it on your salad for lunch, and cook your salmon in it for dinner. Have it readily available in every meal as it can promote better cognitive function and positively influence daily mood.

If olive oil is unavailable, canola oil is a good substitute. Aim to minimize soybean oil as it is the leading source of Omega-6.

PROTEIN

Protein is a vital macromolecule and a major component of diets. However, it is difficult to distinguish the good protein from the bad one.

The items below are the common sources of protein in one's diet.

1. Soy

   Natural soy is healthy. Fermented products have also been proven to be beneficial. These include tamari, miso, natto, and tempeh. Artificial soy may cause a variety of problems.

2. Animal Products

   Organic ones are also considered the best source of protein as they are safer than their counterparts.

   a. Meat of free-roaming animals are considered healthier; it has more omega-3 content and less chemicals. It is also leaner than that of conventionally raised animals, especially when the meat is already processed.
   b. Organic dairy is also better as it is rich in Omega-3 and Vitamin D.
   c. Organic eggs are also better than their counterpart.

To optimize your protein intake, increase your intake of fish meat and decrease that of other animals. Increase your intake of beans, sprouted bread and whey, and casein protein, and decrease that of dairy and eggs. The former sounds actually cheaper than the latter.

MEDITERRANEAN DIET

Modifying what you eat can go a long way into helping you think and feel better. Changes in the diet, such as swapping meat, increasing complex carbohydrates, and consistently using olive oil, can help you attain such goal. These ingredients comprise the Mediterranean Diet, which is commonly observed among the Greeks, Italians and Spaniards.

Another important part of this diet is the predominance of fruits and vegetables. Eating at least seven servings of fruits and vegetables offers not only physical health benefits but also happiness and tranquility.

Fruits and vegetables are rich in vitamins and minerals, which have all been involved in improving one's mood.

1. *Folate*, or Vitamin B9, is widely known to prevent depression. Although fortified processed products like cereal and other grains contain folic acid (synthetic form of folate), it is still best to choose green and leafy vegetables such as spinach and broccoli as they contain the natural folate.
2. *Cobalamin*, or Vitamin B12, also promotes mood, energy, and cognition. It is found in organic eggs and fish.
3. *Vitamin D* promotes calcium absorption. It can also combat depression and can be found in salmon and in fruits and vegetables. To activate the Vitamin D in your body, expose yourself to morning sunshine for fifteen to twenty minutes.

You cannot just substitute vegetables and fruits with pills. Vegetables and fruits have cofactors that are necessary to produce the brain chemicals that carry out certain body processes.

Caffeine is one good example of an antioxidant. It can either be your friend or your foe. The right type and amount of caffeine can positively affect your physical and mental health. It can help prevent cognitive decline. However, using and drinking artificial sources of caffeine (like soda) may fog your brain; adding artificial sweeteners may fog it all the more.

Alcohol is a good antioxidant, too. Like caffeine, the right type and amount of alcohol can prevent cognitive impairment. For women, one glass of it a day may prevent blood sugar spike and counteract toxins in the brain; for men, two glasses a day is advised. Alcohol is an anti-inflammatory agent, too. However, if you have a personal or familial history of alcoholism, it is best to turn away from alcohol as the risks of substance addiction outweigh the benefits.

Three
TOXIC CLOGS

"How can you tell if you cut a really potent fart while in the grocery store? The lady behind you starts checking her eggs."

OVERMEDICATION

Overmedication is rampant nowadays. People feel as though they need to take medications every time they experience anxiety and stress. However, medications for anxiety and stress have been proven to be hazardous in the long run.

These are the common medications that are used by a lot of people:

1. *Antidepressants* – pro-inflammatory; possibly associated with cancer
2. *Antianxiety drugs* – linked with dementia
3. *Attention Deficit drugs* – used as performance enhancers; common among working moms and college students
4. *Antipsychotic medications*, statins, and others – consumed by people whose problems could have been managed by a simple change in lifestyle

These medicinal drugs may not be as dangerous as the illegal ones, but a high dosage of one of these can result to real danger. Side effects may be as mild as sleepiness, or as fatal as death.

People with conditions that are not serious enough to be classified as a disorder are taking such medications, bringing more harm than good to their body. Of course, it's important for you to take them if your condition requires those drugs and the doctor prescribes them. But, for those whose problems can actually be resolved in a natural way, they're better off without those drugs.

There is no lone solution for all the problems that you may face, but there are better and natural alternatives to prescription drugs. Try to do the following:

1. Listen to your emotions and figure out what is wrong with your life. Start working on these one by one.
2. See anxieties and other negativities in a different light. Anxiety can help direct your focus; depression can be a signal for you to change your perception of the world.
3. Find the good things in your life and celebrate them. Looking only at the bad worsens the situation. Allow yourself to see the good and positive vibes will follow.
4. Learn to welcome fear. Don't hide from it. Do not let anything frighten you away from growing and being happy.
5. Learn to utilize other alternatives, such as natural or herbal remedies or other therapies.

ENVIRONMENTAL TOXINS

Learn to recognize toxins in your environment. You may be unconsciously consuming them. These toxins contribute to bodily processes that result to hormonal imbalance, which then results to negative effects on your mood and thinking.

1. Toxic Drinking Water

   Water pollutants are toxins. For one, manganese is correlated to hyperactivity and lower math scores in children. Not all communities filter this metallic element out. Use an activated carbon filter to ensure clean drinking water. Moreover, try to store water in BPA-free plastic containers only, or in glass or stainless steel ones.

2. Cooking Equipment

   Favor cast iron or stainless steel cookware over the nonstick kind as the latter is made from dangerous chemicals.

Opt to cook in low to medium heat if you still prefer to use the material.

3. Stagnant Indoor Air

   Toxins in your home, from dusts to smoke to other particles, not only affects mental ability but also predisposes a person to certain diseases. Clean your home regularly and use a HEPA filter in your systems. Open your windows and bring live plants inside the house. Wash your hands more frequently.

4. Cleaning Products

   Choose cleaning products that are not only nontoxic but also environment-friendly. Be wary of flame-retardants and pesticides.

Four
OTHER LIFESTYLE ADJUSTMENTS

"My mate urinates only once every seven days.
He reckons he's got a week bladder."

PHYSICAL ACTIVITY

Researchers say that the average person has become more and more inactive over the years. This is due to several factors, such as the travel time, sedentary desk jobs, and most especially, technology. From televisions to smart phones to laptops and tablets, people now have more reasons to remain sitting or lying down.

Sedentary lifestyles predispose a person to a variety of lifestyle diseases that can result to obesity and even to cardiovascular diseases. Studies report that people who sit for more than 23 hours a week have up to 64% risk of dying from heart disease than those who sit for less than 11 hours per week. Below are the benefits of exercise:

1. It maintains body weight.
2. It is one of the best mood boosters.
3. It helps in the development of nerve tissues and promotes better thinking.

This does not mean that you have to engage in high-intensity exercises; you just have to engage in low to moderate-intensity exercises regulary. If your home is within walking distance from your work place, the park, or the grocery store, consider walking than riding in a vehicle. You can do these low-intensity exercises as well.

1. Take the stairs instead of the elevator.
2. Walk around the block after lunch or dinner.
3. Walk around as you talk on your phone.
4. When watching TV, move during commercial breaks.
5. Try to use standing desks or have an exercise ball in your office.
6. Park a few meters away from your destination.

7. Have a dog or any other pet that can encourage you to walk.

SLEEP

Sleep is a necessity. It is involved in weight loss and hormonal balance. Sleep also promotes learning and creativity. Inadequate sleep or disturbance in circadian rhythms may negatively affect your mood and thinking.

The world is overflowing with light – from fluorescent bulbs to electronic devices – that the brain has become unsure of the time you need to be asleep or awake. If you sleep late, you may wake up late and fail to expose yourself to sunshine.

You may still be able to function now, but maybe not in the long run. It is vital for you to sleep early and for no less than 8 hours a day. These are the things that enough sleep can do to you:

1. Improve your mood by decreasing cortisol level and increasing dopamine level.
2. Promote weight loss by increasing metabolism.
3. Increase antioxidants in the form of melatonin, which decreases the risk of cancer.

Whenever you are unable to sleep, do not take sleeping pills, prescribed or not. Not only can they harm your body's natural balance, they can also jeopardize your safety from accidents because of their possible side effects. Adjusting your lifestyle is enough to get you back on track. Do not rely on these medications.

If changing your nightly habits is not enough, try any of these:

1. Try cognitive behavioral therapy.
2. Increase intake of foods that are rich in omega-3 DHA, such as seafoods.
3. Take time-release melatonin *supplements* in lower doses.
4. Expose yourself to sunshine the moment you wake up.
5. Change the lighting in your home and utilize special bulbs that you think can help improve your circadian rhythm. Install dimmers in your incandescent lights.

6. Take a nap as necessary. It can help boost your performance.
7. As much as possible, avoid electronic devices.
8. See to it that your room has a lower temperature in the evening, or take a shower before going to bed. It helps optimize restorative sleep.

TECHNOLOGY

As much as technology has connected people over the years, it has brought about a lot of problems.

1. The constant onslaught of stimuli has distracted people more than ever. It has led to the inability to focus on one task at a time, decreasing one's efficiency at work. It has also affected one's relationship and connectivity with people who matter.
2. The so-called *multitasking* has become prevalent. This has led to the inability to focus on what is most important.
3. Social media has increased isolation and the inability to be present in the moment. It has also led to *bad* moods as one keeps seeing the information other people share, whether he likes it or not.

Learn to step away from all these electronic devices and be fully present in the moment. You can start by doing these:

1. Get an internet website blocker to block certain sites that will compel you to waste your precious time.
2. Put some space between you and your phone to prevent yourself from getting distracted.
3. Be more aware. You can do this through meditating and being away from all the electronic devices.

SOCIAL ISOLATION

Social isolation has increased and connectivity has decreased. Aside from the busy lifestyle, the factors below contribute to such problems:

1. People jump from one job to another and move from one home to another.
2. Some people prefer to live alone, and some wait a long while to get married.
3. The number of one's confidants has decreased from at least three people to almost none at all.
4. Many people choose to spend their time on social media over actually hanging out with friends.

Connections (people with people) are important not only to improve your happiness but also to promote your health. They have been linked to a decrease in mortality rate and the preservation of cognitive abilities. You can try a few of these activities to help you connect and decrease isolation today:

1. Ask a special someone on a date or open yourself up to meeting someone.
2. Initiate sex with someone.
3. Tell someone "I love you."
4. Coach a kid's sports team.
5. Cuddle with a person or a pet.
6. Host a party.
7. Join a new group.
8. Plan a vacation with friends.

SPIRITUAL STARVATION

People who believe in religion and spirituality are also slowly decreasing in number. More people choose to not have any religious affiliations at all. However, it is still necessary to cultivate one's spirituality. If you do not believe in a greater Being, you can still be spiritual. An alone time with nature is one way. It can bring really interesting benefits to your mind and body.

Spiritual health can benefit you a lot, especially your brain. It strengthens the prefrontal cortex, improving your mood and thinking, and decreases activity in the parietal lobe, leading to a heightened feeling of oneness. You get the same effects when you are a believer and part of a religion, regardless of what it is. To get started, you can try to do one of the following:

1. Explore different spiritual paths, then find the best one for you.
2. If you do not enjoy being a part of a religious community, try meditating. Meditation can improve your mental health and defend you from cognitive impairment.
3. Spend time with nature, not only to be one with the universe but also to be good in finding the best solutions to your problems.

Five
SPECIAL CASE CONSIDERATIONS

"No one is listening until you fart."

BEING A NEW PARENT

Having a kid is a challenge, especially to single parents, as it can rearrange their focus and divert their attention. Coping with all the changes can be really exhausting.

Having a kid may interfere with your life and make you less productive than you were, but it can also promote development in many areas of your life. To help in coping with parenthood, here are some simple suggestions:

1. Spend time with your kid and learn to be genuinely grateful for having such a blessing in your life. Try to enjoy being a parent.
2. Follow an anti-inflammatory diet to promote your health.
3. Increase your Omega-3 intake to improve mood and cognition.
4. Fight food cravings of processed products and opt to go for natural ones.
5. Engage yourself in several brain exercises; it promotes cognition.
6. Strengthen your spirituality and practice meditation to promote calmness and serenity.
7. Sleep whenever you can.
8. Remember that the challenges you face are merely temporary and that nothing is ever permanent.

BEING AN ELDERLY

Cognitive impairment is common among the older population nowadays. It is that thin line between normal cognitive functioning and dementia. A difficulty in remembering names or locations of objects, in finding the correct word, and in concentrating is a sign of cognitive impairment.

However, this decline in mental ability does not need to become a new norm for people over 65 years old. It should not be taken for granted as cognitive impairment can further progress to dementia. Prevent it from happening.

Take care of your brain by promoting neurogenesis, which you can do through these:

1. Learn something every single day, even after retirement. It can protect the brain from cognitive decline and increase cognitive reserves. Never stop learning.
2. Engage in leisure activities. Have fun. Be sure to be engage in activities that can increase cognition such as reading and gardening. Minimize watching television; it has been proven to cause decline in thinking.
3. Exercise regularly to improve mood, prevent a myriad of diseases, and enhance mental health.
4. Try to engage in some brain training systems. Continue challenging your abilities, and sharpen them.
5. Add the following brain-boosting food into your diet: berries, fish, turmeric, and some spices.

Six
THE BRAIN FOG FIX PROGRAM

*"Why did the toilet paper roll down the hill?
To get to the bottom."*

Dr. Mike Dow aims to provide people with a program (see below) that can combat and prevent brain fog and several other cognitive problems. *The Brain Fog Fix* program is composed of 21 days and divided into three different parts:

- Week 1: The 7-Day *Mood* Revolution
- Week 2: The 7-Day *Energy* Revolution
- Week 3: The 7-Day *Spirit* Revolution

THE 7-DAY MOOD REGULATION

The first week will be divided into diet and cognition. It includes the following changes:

1. Diet
    a. Substitute sugar and artificial sweeteners with natural sweets like fruits and organic yogurt. Make your own all-natural fruit or vegetable juice or smoothie.
    b. Eat complex carbohydrates (barley, oatmeal, flourless and sprouted grain bread, et cetera) instead of processed snacks, nuts instead of chips, and pizza with Portobello mushrooms instead of dough.
    c. Replace fried foods, inorganic meat, most kinds of oil, and other products that have high omega-6 content with organic meat (from grass-fed, pastured, free-roaming animals), dairy, and eggs. Replace your regular oil with olive oil, canola oil, or flaxseed oil.

d. Decrease your intake of caffeine, alcohol, and other substances that can influence your hormone levels. Have at most two small cups of coffee and one serving of alcohol a day. Do not take recreational drugs. Do not smoke. Try not to take excess prescription medications, or try not to take any medication at all.
e. Add at least one omega-3 superfood, such as fish meat, to your diet per day.
f. Have at least seven servings of vegetables and whole fruits and drink at least TEN 8-ounce glasses of water daily.

2. Cognition

Pay special attention to the following thought patterns that can make you feel bad. Negative thinking will always have a negative effect on your mood. If you catch yourself starting to give in to these thoughts, drive yourself to turn them into something positive. This awareness is the first step into changing the way you think.

a. Personalization – thinking that you are the cause of a certain circumstance
b. Pervasiveness – making a problem affects other parts of your life
c. Paralysis-analysis – getting trapped in your own thoughts
d. Pessimism – always thinking about the negative side of things
e. Polarization – seeing only the *either-or* of a situation
f. Psychic – making assumptions of the thoughts of another person
g. Permanence – allowing the past and present experiences to judge the future

THE 7-DAY ENERGY REVOLUTION

This next phase involves getting your energy levels revved up, so that you will be ready to meet the daily demands of your life.

1. Catch up on sleep and regulate your circadian rhythm by going to bed at 11:00pm and waking up at 7:00am every day. Ensure the environment is conducive to sleep and expose yourself to sunlight the moment you wake up.
2. Exercise for at least 44 minutes per day.
3. Expose yourself to challenges and learn new things every day. It can stimulate brain activity. Do some leisurely activities and try out new ones.
4. Extend your attention span by not watching TV or any form of online entertainment. Watch movies in the theater only. Refrain from social media and move away from electronic devices within your waking hours.

THE 7-DAY SPIRIT REVOLUTION

This phase will strengthen your prefrontal cortex and your connections with the people around you. Consider these:

1. Find out your meaning and purpose in life by reflecting.
2. Feel connected by joining a religious community or a spiritual practice. Strengthen your bond with nature and animals. Try to have a philosophical, political, or scientific awareness of a larger world. Meditate or pray; either of these can help you maximize connectedness.

The 7-Day Mood Revolution can help resolve problems with mood and thinking. The 7-Day Energy Revolution can help combat laziness and problems with energy levels. And the 7-Day Spirit Revolution can help prevent feelings of disconnectedness or detachment.

Follow the regimen strictly. However, it is safe to say that it may not be possible to follow this systematic plan for the rest of your life. So, try to follow it 80% of the time or whenever you need the boost.

Good luck!

Seven
ANALYSIS

"What did one toilet say to the other toilet? You look flushed."

Dr. Mike Dow provides an interesting approach to one of the most common concerns of adults nowadays. He breaks away from the conventions of the medicine world, and his book, *The Brain Fog Fix*, promotes simple lifestyle changes for improved cognitive health. An anecdote precedes the explanation of each chapter, allowing it to be relatable to the readers.

The Brain Fog Fix gives a ton of information, yet the medical jargons are easy to comprehend, showing the obvious effort of *Dr. Mike Dow.*

The Brain Fog Fix is organized very well. First, it provides the readers with the *whats* and *whys* before the program is offered. The examples are relevant and every claim is backed up by a scientific study.

The Brain Fog Fix program sounds easy to implement. Everything is widely available at home. You can simply get started whenever you choose to.

Eight
A READER'S GUIDE

"Since writing on toilet walls is done neither for critical acclaim nor financial reward, it's the purest form of fart."

Now that you've finished reading the summary, take some time to ponder the learnings that you have acquired. You can recommend this short summary to a fellow creator, so that you will have someone to talk to about it. Or you can discuss it with colleagues and friends who have already read the summary and who have always desired to pursue the arts. Discuss your thoughts and your learnings with one another.

Use these questions as your guide:

1. How often do you get irritated, tired, and busy?

2. Think about your food intake in a week. What do you usually eat? Do you think it has a big influence on your mood?

3. Do you take medications to help you relax, focus, or fall asleep?

4. How do you describe your sleep patterns now?

5. How often do you engage in social media? Are you one of those people who get tied to their seats once Facebook site is opened? Are you one of those people who meet friends at a coffee shop but do not talk with one another as their eyes are glued on their phones? Has it helped you stay connected?

Advice from Bern:

Take TEN more minutes as you allow this book to change your life. Write down the concepts that have spiked your interest and reread them tomorrow. That's it.

Give *The Brain Fog Fix* a chance to change your life. Follow the program and notice how your mood and your thinking change over the weeks.

Changing your mind can change your life, and changing your mind is simpler than it seems, as long as you allow it.

I hope *Dr. Mike Dow*'s *The Brain Fog Fix* is the book you have always been waiting for.

Best of luck!

~~ May you never be the same ~~

Content Contribution | Jessa Tocaldo, Epiphany Printing
Cover | Junry dela Torre, BLVNP, Incorporated
Editing | Karen Lechoco & Elle Carradine, BLVNP, Incorporated

Check out ONE of my *BEST-SELLING and LIFE-CHANGING* summaries.

From the original book by *Dan Buettner*, *The Blue Zones Solution*, this summary will teach you how to eat and live like the world's healthiest people.

You will learn the series of small nudges that will come a long way into transforming your life. Travel around the world with this interesting book and discover the secret to a happy, healthy, and long life.

START LIVING AND EATING HEALTHY NOW!

This summary will help you:

- Learn how the Blue Zones Project works.
- Reach and survive 100 years old.
- Transform your lifestyle the Blue Zone way.
- Eat better and move more with a happy and stress-less life.
- Influence your community into becoming a Blue Zone.
- Choose healthy and non-toxic foods.
- Prepare healthier meals for you and your family
- Start making a delicious and healthy meal in minutes

Why you MUST READ this summary?

I want you to be healthy, too! Living a healthy life is more than just will power and discipline. It is also about influencing an environment and everyone around you to develop and maintain a healthy lifestyle. Learn to celebrate life; start with your household and influence your community. You will be surprised by how easy being healthy can be.

Check out another ONE of my *BEST-SELLING* and *LIFE-CHANGING* summaries.

Are you ready to lose up to TWENTY pounds in just FOUR weeks?

In just TEN minutes, you will have the knowledge necessary in attaining a glorious bod. You can start investing in your health. You will invest in your health because you want to be healthy.

So, INVEST IN YOUR HEALTH NOW!

This summary will help you:

- Maintain or repair your metabolism.
- Learn the effects of stress on your body and the ways to prevent it.
- Learn how to avoid certain foods that damage your metabolism.
- Learn the importance of a healthy metabolism in attaining your ideal body weight.
- Find certain exercises that fit into the phases of the plan.
- Learn how the phases of *The Fast Metabolism Diet* complement your body's needs.
- Learn the common dieting routines that harm your body.
- Know the importance of the perfect timing of food intake.
- Know the effects of eating healthy foods on your body and your mood.

Why you MUST READ this summary?

The Fast Metabolism Diet plan of *Haylie Pomroy* can satisfy your body's caloric requirements and allow you to enjoy your favorite dishes, even as you try to shed off those extra pounds.

A 28-day cycle, *The Fast Metabolism Diet* is an effective and fresh plan that perfectly complements your body's needs, so that you are able to ingest your daily dietary requirements, with the added benefits of stabilizing your blood sugar, increasing your energy levels, improving your sleep, and reducing your stress.

Have you ever noticed that you are being lured into the digital world more than you like?

Sometimes, it is for personal reasons; sometimes, it is for your business - to keep it alive and growing.

That is why putting your gadgets down, gripping your crayons, and landing them on paper are the best things you can do for yourself.

Coloring is a physical activity that activates different parts of your brain, parts that are necessary for the development of your skills. It may be hard to step away from the screen, and the withdrawal symptoms may be tough albeit unnoticeable, but having your *Coloring Book* at hand can help ease those, leave you refreshed, and help you get ready to tackle more work later on.

Enjoy coloring these dream manifestation patterns!

• This *Adult Coloring Book* features over TEN intricately detailed patterns.

• The designs range in complexity, from beginner to expert level.

• This provides you with hours of relief, mindful calm, and fun and creative expression.

My latest book, *A Manifestation and Dream Journal*, is inspired by the wonderful patterns in the "*Adult Coloring Book: Stress Relieving Patterns*" by *Blue Star Coloring*. As a young adult who can empathize with people who go through many adversities, I can say that the illustrators of *Blue Star Coloring* have perfectly designed an *Adult Coloring Book* that is meant to relieve stress and shoo all those negative vibes away.

Join millions of adults, all around the world, who are rediscovering the simple relaxation and joy of coloring with my *Coloring Book, A Manifestation and Dream Journal*!

It is more than just a coloring book; it is your guide to realizing your dreams. :)

Look for A Manifestation and Dream Journal

on Amazon!

~ *Also by* **Bern Bolo** ~

Summary of these famous books:

The 21 Irrefutable Laws of Leadership

Extreme Ownership

The Five Dysfunctions of a Team

Big Magic

Essentialism

You Are a Badass

Rising Strong

The Charisma Myth

Getting to Yes

The 7-Day Flat-Belly Tea Cleanse

Mindset

No Sweat

Confident You

Blackout

The End of Jobs

All the Single Ladies

Adios, America

The 4-Hour Workweek

Grey

The Wright Brothers

Elon Musk

Becoming Steve Jobs

Tidying Up

The E-Myth Revisited

6 Months to 6 Figures

Factory Man

Flash Boys

About the Author

A year ago, I was so ignorant that I did not even know how to copy-and-paste. I did not know what net income and gross profit were or what a profit cycle meant. BUT...

My spirit kept leading me to the world of business. I wanted to be in it so much and I didn't know how. Yet, it did not matter. One of the cardinal things that I have learned from all my experiences: once you have the courage and the right drive, you are halfway to your dreams.

At first, I just dreamed of becoming a businessperson. I strived hard, and by reading LOTS and lots of business books, like Zero to One, The One Minute Manager, Cashflow Quadrant, Unfair Advantage, and more, I received epiphany after epiphany. Now, my dreams are a reality. Now, I am in the arena.

Only ONE YEAR later, I have established a profitable business and I have provided opportunities to many people, who are now working for me.
Sometimes, I look back and connect the dots of my past to those of my present. I have accomplished what I used to think was impossible to reach. And that never fails to amaze me. Who would have thought that reading these books could change my life? Books, indeed, are one of the most powerful things a man can hold.

I AM SO LUCKY to realise that soon enough. I was only dreaming many years before, until a year ago.

For my reader, I wish you greater success than I have ever had, in even less time. I wish for Epiphany Printing to open your eyes and mind, and fortify your will and spirit, so that you, too, can see how abundant the world is...

So that you, too, can see the opportunities that you never thought existed and realize that they are right there, next to you.

Through my writings, let your spirit wake up. Be who you want to be. You are so lucky. You always have been. Keep thinking that, and you will get luckier. :)

26756931R00029

Made in the USA
San Bernardino, CA
03 December 2015